VALERIA HUGHES

Fresh Fire, Miracles & Kings

Transformative Conversations from the book of Acts

First Published by Kingdom Advance 2026

First edition

ISBN: 979-8-9892898-4-4

This book was professionally typeset on Atticus.

Contents

Introduction

Welcome to the Small Group Series!

There is such a powerful connection when people meet in small groups to think deeply, discuss scripture and their walk with Jesus.

Some reasons for gathering:

- Ignite Kingdom Purpose through intellectually challenging questions and Bible-based conversations
- To build community across the body of Christ through intentional discourse
- To bring generations together in unity

As you gather the group for this important conversation about the book of Acts, work to be vulnerable and open-minded. The best times are when we take the roof off and the walls down.

Bring your Bible but also bring along a big boatload of trust and some buckets of mercy.

The intention is to equip churches with the resources necessary for the end-time harvest. Thanks for coming along on this journey!

Instructions for Small-Group Discussions

Nitty-Gritty of all the things

Welcome to the most inspirational type of learning—group discussion!

Group discussions through weekly or monthly groups are a fascinating way to build a solid, foundational basis of the local church. Meeting together in a house was foundational to the early church in the book of Acts.

The disciples and members of the body of Christ met on a regular basis, from house to house. House groups are truly more like the early church than even our modern church services.

Work with your pastor to get a house group together and follow along on the journey of the thirteen group discussions. Grab some sour dough bread, cheese, chocolate, and fruit for a simple charcuterie board, maybe some hot tea, and the table is set for the meeting.

This study has THIRTEEN lessons. So, plenty of content for 12-13 weeks or months. The study could be once a month for a year. Or the study could be for a quarter if the group is to meet each week.

This study material is designed for each participant **to have and to hold their own copy of the book**—either printed copy or kindle version.

Each lesson contains:

- Ice breaker—to move everyone to the same page and wavelength for the session
- Focus and Scripture Text
- Lesson—usually about four paragraphs in length. Could be augmented to be longer but that length is really all the lecture that is necessary.
- Discussion questions—once the group works to craft a group covenant, aka group guidelines, this portion will be the most exciting piece of the week. If all participants have the study guide, everyone is encouraged to take time to ponder and reflect on the questions for the week or month in between the group session. This could be added to each participant's daily devotional time as additional study and thought.
- Take-Aways or Closure in prayer—this is a time to hear a last word from everyone in the group and to collectively pray together. Corporate prayer times usually greatly enhance the group's time together as the Word and Spirit are sealed, cemented together.
- Self-Reflection for the Week—a place for each member of the group to reflect on the week's study, either before the study or after the study. Or both!

Leading a Group Discussion

Leading a group discussion is a finely-honed skill that takes time. That skill requires the leader to be and humble. Arrogance on the part of the leader will only lead to extreme frustration of the participants. If the leader works to be vulnerable and open, the group will mirror the leader.

NOTE: If this is your first time leading a group, tell yourself that you are the guide on the side. you are not the center stage act at each group session. There is to be NO special chair for the leader or anything preposterous like that. Group discussions are meant to function as walking through life together, not to watch a leader make a spectacle of him or herself. Honesty and humbleness is the key factor.

The leader must not be afraid to be transparent and vulnerable for the group. This will create a safe space. The job of the leader is to create a safe space for all participants. To make sure each participant has equal voice and equal participation in each session.

The job of the leader might be asking the more introverted people to prepare to provide a response for the next question. Vice versa, the leader's job is also to gently assist the over-eager extroverts to not monopolize every response.

The ones to watch for the are those 'sneak-a-preach' garden varieties. These create a challenge for the leader but with care and gentleness, everyone will eventually realize how important the shared time and space is and will proceed with respect and honor for the group discussions.

Some strategies to move along any discussion are as follows:

- Asking clarifying questions to persuade the speaker to continue talking or explaining his/her thoughts
- Rephrasing what the participant said as active listening
- Adding onto the participant's answer or response to the question such as: I also think, I agree, I disagree and here's why, have you thought of xyz..., that reminds me,
- Connecting the discussion back to previous week's discussion or other questions or topics, even books or podcasts
- Follow-up questions to move the conversation into more critical thinking, rather than only surface level learning or feeling
- Recognize and acknowledge differences in the room
- Make the space a safe place for everyone to participate
- Gently help someone who has overshared to allow other more introverted participants to have a chance to speak

Group Guidelines, AKA Group Covenant

Most of our church attendees are normalized to passive learning. Participation mostly means shaking hands or singing together. This means that they can sit in silence all throughout the church service and observe the proceedings without much input. While this works for a lecture format, this style really hinders the discussion style format.

Discussion groups move everyone to the forefront of the shared workload.

These groups offer all participants the chance to speak, think deeply about the Word of God, debate, agree and disagree. To make sure this happens every time the group meets, the group must set guidelines from the beginning.

Setting the group guidelines together, during the first meeting, will enhance the unity and cohesion of the group dynamics. In order to do this, ask every participant to share what they expect and need from the discussion group. If this meeting is conducted correctly, the majority of time will be spent on the creation of the group covenant and the distribution of the study books, making the length of the group fourteen weeks.

When groups have a well-planned beginning and conclusion, the outcome will be a spectacular one that will be repeated in the near future. If the leader or the group just decides to get together and haphazardly reads questions in a monotonous voice, the outcome will be downright pitiful.

Appoint a scribe to take notes. Even better, collaborate as the group builds the group guidelines on a marker board or large pieces of poster board or extra large post-it notes.

Work together to build the group guidelines:

- Method of communication text, texting app such as WhatsApp or other
- Time to meet—must work for every single participant
- Time of worship or not
- Time to finish the discussion—non-negotiable for the host's sake

- How to handle the inevitable conflict that will arise
- How often and where to meet each time if alternating host sites
- When to eat—before or after the group discussion
- What to eat—lite snacks, sweet/salty, full meals, desserts only, etc.
- Food on a rotating schedule, everyone brings something every time, etc.
- Babysitting discussion—this one is tricky

A job for each person: communicator for the week, note taker, attendance recorder, prayer leader, bathroom cleaner, assist the host with set-up, food clean-up, drinks, ice, children's activity, etc. All could also be on a revolving schedule, but the group must decide this and appoint the scheduler of tasks.

Barriers to Good Discussion

Every group will experience a few awkward moments in the beginning. That is to be expected. Once the entire group establishes the group guidelines, all participants will know exactly what to do and what to expect. If any one person is permitted to disrupt the group dynamics, the entire group will crumble and fall apart. The reason? When trust is broken, trust is almost impossible to rebuild in a group setting. Take the time to process the guidelines.

Svinicki and McKeachie (2001, pp. 44-45) discuss five barriers to good discussion:

1. Habits of lifelong church attendance usually mean passive learning
2. Fear of appearing stupid
3. Trying too hard to find the answer the 'leader' is looking for
4. Failing to see value in the discussion topic or process
5. Wanting to settle on a solution before considering alternatives.

Size of Group

Most cohesive and effective small groups are anywhere from 6 to 12 attendees. Of course, the more people in the group, the more discussion time is needed. Vice versa.

For maximum participation, discussion groups need to be eight people or fewer. To make this happen, the larger group could break into two groups. At the conclusion, a leader from each group could summarize any pertinent points to the larger group.

Small-group studies are the perfect place to invite new folks. It's usually non-threatening and a less formal event than a weekend church service. If groups grow beyond 12-16 people, the group then splits into two new groups to meet in two different places.

There is a lot of information about small-group ministry online, and when and how to split the groups most naturally. This book's purpose is specifically only content and how to effectively lead/participate in a small-group study with discussion questions.

Lesson One: Jerusalem

The Lord Jesus birthed the church that He designed to grow

Focus Thought

The Lord Jesus gave birth to a church that He designed to grow and emerge as a dynamic, proactive, mission-minded, consecrated, passionate, and powerful organism.

Focus Verse

Acts 1:8, New King James Version

But you shall receive power when the Holy Spirit has come upon you; and you shall be witnesses to Me in Jerusalem, and in all Judea and Samaria, and to the end of the earth."

Background Notes for the Group Facilitator

Conduct some research of your own with these internet websites concerning the Temple Mount and the Dome of the Rock:

www.templemount.org

bibleplaces.com/templemount

Suggested Meeting Schedule

Open with Prayer Icebreaker (5 minutes)

Optional Worship Session (5-10 minutes)

Lesson (5-10 minutes)

Discussion (20-30 minutes)

Wrap-up and Reflection (10 minutes)

Share Prayer Needs for the Week

Close with Prayer

Icebreaker (5 minutes)

Tell someone of your new birth experience into the church. Where did it occur? When? What was the story leading up to the experience?

Leader: Encourage group members to get their testimony in written form to share with unbelievers. More information on this in the appendix.

Lesson (5-10 minutes)

Jesus' ministry began with his baptism by John the Baptist in the Jordan River three years prior to His arrival arrival in Jerusalem. Many events occurred throughout the three years of Jesus' ministry: calling the twelve disciples, healing the sick, calming angry seas, casting out demonic spirits, preaching the gospel, and teaching in the synagogues.

Jerusalem was the location where Jesus' ministry culminated. (See Matthew 16:21.) Jesus entered ministry with the end in mind. He understood the purpose of His coming: to suffer and die for the sins of the world. (See Mark 10:45.)

Jerusalem's temple has much historical significance. King Solomon built a temple which served as the one location that was ordained of God. The people brought their tithes and offerings to the temple and the Lord ordained that it was the place of His holy habitation. The presence of the Lord dwelt in the temple until Jesus Christ died on the cross. God never forgot His people. Even today, the Temple Mount in Jerusalem is a holy place of worship.

The Holy Ghost was first poured out in Jerusalem in Acts 2:1-11. Acts 1:8 states that the disciples were to be witnesses in Jerusalem first and then to all near and distant lands. Jerusalem was the location of these events the very place and people that had rejected and crucified Him. (See Matthew 23:3.)

Today, three monotheistic religions claim Jerusalem to be their Holy City: Jews, Muslims, and Christians.

Acts 1:1-12, New King James Version

1 The former account I made, O Theophilus, of all that Jesus began both

to do and teach,

2 until the day in which He was taken up, after He through the Holy Spirit had given commandments to the apostles whom He had chosen,

3 to whom He also presented Himself alive after His suffering by many infallible proofs, being seen by them during forty days and speaking of the things pertaining to the kingdom of God.

4 And being assembled together with them, He commanded them not to depart from Jerusalem, but to wait for the Promise of the Father, "which," He said, "you have heard from Me;

5 for John truly baptized with water, but you shall be baptized with the Holy Spirit not many days from now."

6 Therefore, when they had come together, they asked Him, saying, "Lord, will You at this time restore the kingdom to Israel?"

7 And He said to them, "It is not for you to know times or seasons which the Father has put in His own authority.

8 But you shall receive power when the Holy Spirit has come upon you; and you shall be witnesses to Me in Jerusalem, and in all Judea and Samaria, and to the end of the earth."

9 Now when He had spoken these things, while they watched, He was taken up, and a cloud received Him out of their sight.

10 And while they looked steadfastly toward heaven as He went up, behold, two men stood by them in white apparel,

11 who also said, "Men of Galilee, why do you stand gazing up into heaven? This same Jesus, who was taken up from you into heaven, will so come in like manner as you saw Him go into heaven."

12 Then they returned to Jerusalem from the mount called Olivet, which

is near Jerusalem, a Sabbath day's journey.

Discussion (20-30 minutes)

1. Read Acts 1:1-12. Discuss the actual modern-day locations mentioned in the passage while looking at a biblical map of that time period.

2. Discuss why Jesus chose for the city of Jerusalem to be the place of choice for His chosen people.

3. Read Acts 1:8. Discuss the geographical aspects of that command. Did Jesus want His followers to keep the power in Jerusalem? Why or why not?

4. The history surrounding the temple in Jerusalem is one of triumph and tragedy. God outlined a clear plan for blessing and favor but unfortunately, the Jewish people did not always follow God's commands. The Old Testament is filled with examples and stories of the Gentiles giving in to idol worship and other practices that went against its' teaching. The Gentiles suffered at the hands of many nations because of disobedience and arrogance. Discuss this history in light of the outpouring in Jerusalem in Acts 1. Why is this significant?

5. Read II Chronicles 6:6. Discuss the reasons that God choose Jerusalem. Read also Deuteronomy 12:5-7, 11-12; Psalm 132:13; and Psalm 78:68.

6. The birth of the apostolic church was in the upper room in the city of Jerusalem. Discuss this heritage.

7. Read Matthew 16:18. Discuss what the Lord meant by "upon this

rock."

8. The Dome of the Rock, placed on the Temple Mount, is a place of Islamic worship today. Some theorize that both the temple that Solomon built and the Holy of Holies sit directly underneath the Dome of the Rock. Discuss how Jerusalem can be the home to these three monotheistic religions: Jews, Muslims, and Christians.

9. Sometimes, it seems that God chooses the most obscure places to fulfill His promises. Compare these obscure places: foreign fields, the inner-city ghettos, a maximum-security prison and the unlikelihood of the upper room in Jerusalem.

Reflection and Wrap-Up

Just as the church has its beginnings in Jerusalem, every Christian also has its beginning. Are you grateful for your beginning with Jesus or is it an event that you take for granted?

Have you given proper credit to those individuals most responsible for your humble beginning as a Christian or your precipice in ministry?

Just as we rejoice in the upper room experience that began in Jerusalem, we must also rejoice in our first upper room experience. What could you do in your own personal life to honor those most responsible for your conversion or your experience?

Start now living a life of thankfulness to the Lord for the rich heritage that you enjoy.

Thank the Lord for the birth of the church in Acts 1 and for you new birth.

Folks with hearts of gratitude never have trouble remembering their heritage and their humble beginnings.

Take five minutes of this quiet, reflective time to examine your heart while the music plays softly.

Take five minutes for prayer needs. Discuss group ministry projects.

Close with prayer. Encourage each participant to work through the reflection that follows this page.

Optional: Time of fellowship with light snacks.

Reflection for this week

Write your thoughts about this week's lesson:

Explain your thoughts about any specific points from the discussion:

Perhaps you have thought of another question you'd love to ask the group next time? Write it here so you don't forget.

Copy down one or two scriptures from scripture text from the lesson: You may copy the scripture from any of your favorite versions of the Bible.

Lesson Two: Coming of the Spirit

The promised outpouring of the Spirit was fulfilled

Focus Thought

Jesus fulfilled His promise that the Holy Ghost would come upon His followers.

Focus Verse

Acts 1:4-5, New King James Version

4 And being assembled together with them, He commanded them not to depart from Jerusalem, but to wait for the Promise of the Father, "which," He said, "you have heard from Me;

5 for John truly baptized with water, but you shall be baptized with the

Holy Spirit not many days from now."

Background Notes for the Group Facilitator

Pray fervently that the group will catch the fire of the Holy Ghost and be consumed with the fire for their personal revival.

Pray that the group will be fervent with personal evangelism after this lesson concerning the Holy Ghost outpouring.

Suggested Meeting Schedule

Open with Prayer

Icebreaker (5 minutes)

Optional Worship Session (5-10 minutes)

Lesson (5-10 minutes)

Discussion (20-30 minutes)

Wrap-up and Reflection (10 minutes)

Share Prayer Needs for the Week

Close with Prayer

Icebreaker (5 minutes)

Tell the group about a promise that someone made to you as a child and kept. How did it make you feel? If that person had broken the promise, how would you have felt?

Lesson (5-10 minutes)

Jesus' death on Calvary was the ultimate sacrifice for sin. However, the focal point of God's plan of redemption was the infilling of the Holy Ghost. Acts 2:38 states that a person must repent of their sins, be baptized in the name of Jesus for the remission of sins, and be filled with the Holy Ghost. The gift of the Holy Ghost completes the new birth by giving the believer new life and the ability to rise above sin and to live a rich life, full of promise.

God's plan to save mankind has two interesting components: the power to destroy sin and to transform the sinner into one who would inhabit His righteousness. (See II Corinthians 5:21.) God took upon the sins of the world so we would be righteous and holy. He defeated the powers of darkness so the church could be transformed. (See Isaiah 53:4-5; Galatians 3:13.)

Jesus proclaimed that the disciples would be filled with the Holy Ghost before He ascended into heaven. (See Acts 1:5.) The prophet Joel had prophesied that God would pour out His Spirit upon all flesh in Joel 2:28. When Peter preached the induction message in the upper room, he referred to Joel's prophecy and boldly stated that his prophecy would be fulfilled that day. (See Acts 2:39.)

The Holy Spirit changed the landscape of the world from the moment it arrived. Thousands had gathered in Jerusalem to celebrate the Feast of Pentecost when the Holy Ghost was poured out upon 120 believers. (See Acts 2:1-4.) The Jews had long awaited this promise, and it had arrived with a powerful display. (See Isaiah 28:11.)

The Spirit had arrived, and many would soon realize that it would change the very face of the world because of its power and glory. Over the course of ensuing decades, many lives would be transformed by its dramatic power and undeniable personal experience.

Acts 2:1-4, 14-21, 37-40, New King James Version

1 When the Day of Pentecost had fully come, they were all with one accord in one place.

2 And suddenly there came a sound from heaven, as of a rushing mighty wind, and it filled the whole house where they were sitting.

3 Then there appeared to them divided tongues, as of fire, and one sat upon each of them.

4 And they were all filled with the Holy Spirit and began to speak with other tongues, as the Spirit gave them utterance.

14 But Peter, standing up with the eleven, raised his voice and said to them, "Men of Judea and all who dwell in Jerusalem, let this be known to you, and heed my words.

15 For these are not drunk, as you suppose, since it is only the third hour of the day.

16 But this is what was spoken by the prophet Joel:

17 'And it shall come to pass in the last days, says God, That I will pour out of My Spirit on all flesh; Your sons and your daughters shall prophesy, Your young men shall see visions, Your old men shall dream dreams.

18 And on My menservants and on My maidservants I will pour out My Spirit in those days; And they shall prophesy.

19 I will show wonders in heaven above And signs in the earth beneath: Blood and fire and vapor of smoke.

20 The sun shall be turned into darkness, And the moon into blood, Before the coming of the great and awesome day of the Lord.

21 And it shall come to pass That whoever calls on the name of the Lord Shall be saved.'

37 Now when they heard this, they were cut to the heart, and said to Peter and the rest of the apostles, "Men and brethren, what shall we do?"

38 Then Peter said to them, "Repent, and let every one of you be baptized in the name of Jesus Christ for the remission of sins; and you shall receive the gift of the Holy Spirit.

39 For the promise is to you and to your children, and to all who are afar off, as many as the Lord our God will call."

40 And with many other words he testified and exhorted them, saying, "Be saved from this perverse generation."

Discussion (20-30 minutes)

1. Read Acts 2:1-4. Discuss the arrival of the Holy Spirit and its physical manifestation.
2. Read Acts 2:14-21. Discuss the certainty that Peter preached about Joel's prophecy coming to pass—that very day.
3. Read Acts 2:37-40. Discuss what the people had heard that made them feel such conviction. Peter spoke with much clarity in Acts 2:38-39. Why is this scripture still relevant to the church today?
4. Describe the faith that the 120 must have possessed to tarry in the upper room until the promise was fulfilled. Would we have that kind of faith in today's world? Why or why not?

5. In Luke 24:49, Jesus told His disciples to tarry in Jerusalem until they are endued with power from on high. Do you think that the disciples had any idea of the magnitude of what they were about to receive? Discuss.

6. How did the upper room experience become a social and cultural revival in Jerusalem and all the uttermost parts of the earth?

7. Discuss how the disciples were transformed from timid, scared men to bold evangelists. How was the power of the Holy Ghost at work in their lives to bring about this change?

8. If all the supernatural were removed from the book of Acts, what would be left? What happens in a person or in the local church if the supernatural is removed or not allowed to work? Why?

9. How has the Holy Ghost transformed your life? Are the fruits of the Spirit in action in your life? (See Galatians 5:22-23.)

Reflection and Wrap-Up

Are you living a transformed life?

Are you living and preaching a bold message just like the apostles did in the book of Acts? Why or why not?

The Holy Ghost is for everyone: all nationalities, all socioeconomic strata, and all cultures. How are you proclaiming the coming of the Holy Ghost to your world?

Are you still expecting the promise of the Father in your family, your friends, your co-workers, your neighbors?

Have you forgotten about the promise in Joel 2:28? What are you personally doing to have a book of Acts experience in your own life?

Take five minutes of this quiet, reflective time to examine your heart while the music plays softly.

Take a moment for the prayer needs of the group.

Close with prayer. Encourage each participant to work through the reflection that follows this page.

Optional: Time of fellowship with light snacks.

Reflection for this week

Write your thoughts about this week's lesson:

Explain your thoughts about any specific points from the discussion:

Perhaps you have thought of another question you'd love to ask the group next time? Write it here so you don't forget

Lesson Three: The Early Church in Focus

Individual believers were the focus of the New Testament church.

Focus Thought

Individual believers frame the early church's membership. They remain as God's focus throughout the New Testament.

Focus Verse

Acts 2:38, New King James Version

Then Peter said to them, "Repent, and let every one of you be baptized in the name of Jesus Christ for the remission of sins; and you shall receive the gift of the Holy Spirit.

Background Notes for the Group Facilitator

Ask your church leadership for the names of the most recent guests and the newest converts. At the conclusion of the questions, the group will be asked to problem-solve how to better build relationships between the three groups: members, new converts, and guests.

Suggested Meeting Schedule

Open with Prayer

Icebreaker (5 minutes)

Optional Worship Session (5-10 minutes)

Lesson (5-10 minutes)

Discussion (20-30 minutes)

Wrap-up and Reflection (10 minutes)

Share Prayer Needs for the Week

Close with Prayer

Icebreaker (5 minutes)

Think about your relationship with your grandparents. Bring a photo of your grandparents and be ready to share a story of something they taught you about life.

How did your grandparents teach you about relationships? Explain.

Lesson (5-10 minutes)

The church is in the people business. The church is a social organization—the focus is on people, all kinds of people. Jesus focused on people and social functions. His first miracle was at a wedding in Cana. (See John 2:1-11.)

Jesus visited the temple and the synagogues. He taught people in every type of setting. He built a team of men into a world-changing ministering force. His teaching was filled with examples about people. Jesus sought the unpopular: Zacchaeus, the woman at the well, and the man by the pool of Bethesda. Jesus ministered to individuals. (See Luke 12:6-7, John 3:1-21 and John 4:4-30.)

Within the Great Commission, Jesus had two important points: baptize and teach. (See Matthew 28:19.) He presented a need to evangelize the world and to teach the new converts important doctrinal messages. (See Mark 16:15-16.)

The first church was fierce in its determination to reach the lost world. They fulfilled the Lord's commission with great zeal and passion. (See Acts 5:42; Acts 8:4, 25; 11:20; 14:21; 28:31.)

The kingdom is all about people—building relationships and evangelizing every creature. As the church, we cannot discriminate on account of age, socioeconomic level, or financial stability.

Individuals who enjoy living a reclusive lifestyle would not make credible disciples of Jesus. The first church reached people of every sort through its evangelism. We must allow our converted, resurrected hearts to bring hope to another heart that feels without hope. Jesus was in the people business, and so should we, the church.

Acts 2:38-40, New King James Version

38 Then Peter said to them, "Repent, and let every one of you be baptized in the name of Jesus Christ for the remission of sins; and you shall receive the gift of the Holy Spirit.
39 For the promise is to you and to your children, and to all who are afar off, as many as the Lord our God will call."
40 And with many other words, he testified and exhorted them, saying, "Be saved from this perverse generation."

Matthew 10:30, NKJV

30 But the very hairs of your head are all numbered.

Luke 21:34, 36, NKJV

34 "But take heed to yourselves, lest your hearts be weighed down with carousing, drunkenness, and cares of this life, and that Day come on you unexpectedly.

36 Watch therefore, and pray always that you may be counted worthy to escape all these things that will come to pass, and to stand before the Son of Man."

Colossians 1:27, NKJV

27 To them God willed to make known what are the riches of the glory of this mystery among the Gentiles: which is Christ in you, the hope of

glory.

Philippians 2:12, NKJV

12 Therefore, my beloved, as you have always obeyed, not as in my presence only, but now much more in my absence, work out your own salvation with fear and trembling;

Discussion (20-30 minutes)

1. Read Acts 2:38-40. Discuss this great, timeless promise.
2. Read Matthew 10:30 and Luke 21:34, 36. Explain how these verses can be compared together.
3. Read Colossians 1:27 and Philippians 2:12. Describe how our hope must be taken care of on an individual basis.
4. Locate examples in your Bibles of how Jesus reached people. Work in pairs if desired. Report back to the group when finished.
5. Discuss all the modern technology that we have at our fingertips. Discuss how technology makes us better or worse communicators.
6. God is concerned about people. You might have heard this well-worn adage, "People don't care how much you know unless they know how much you care." Compare this adage with the concept that God is concerned about people. How are they alike? Different?
7. God has provided His people a guidebook for relationships. Read

these scriptures and discuss God's way of handling people: Ephesians 4:29; Matthew 5:44-48; John 13:34-35; 15:17.

8. Read these examples of Jesus ministering to people and discuss how those same situations would look today. Read John 8; Luke 18:18-23; Mark 10 and Luke 18:15-16.

9. What are some ways that your local church can strengthen the relationships between the members, new converts, and guests? TIP: Use the lists of names provided by your group leader to lead the session of problem-solving.

Reflection and Wrap-Up

Take a moment to think about how God really loves people. Consider how much He loves you. Jesus came to this earth to die on a cross for the sins of people. He gave His very life so that all others could live free from condemnation.

How are your relationships? Are they following the principles set forth in the Word that guide relationships? Are there some fences that need repairing in your life? Are there some distant family members that God is calling you to show mercy upon?

We will be judged in our treatment of people. Are you prejudiced? Do you show favoritism at church or within your own family? God thinks that is wrong. Pray right now for God to reveal to your heart and mind any repairs that need to be made to your relationships.

How is your relationship with the Creator? Is sin separating you from Him? Repent today. Get right, and then go and find someone to tell about Jesus and His great redemption plan.

Take a moment

Take five minutes of this quiet, reflective time to examine your heart while the music plays softly.

Take five minutes for prayer needs.

Close with prayer. Encourage each participant to work through the reflection that follows this page.

Optional: Time of fellowship with light snacks.

Reflection for this week

Write your thoughts about this week's lesson:

Explain your thoughts about any specific points from the discussion:

Perhaps you have thought of another question you'd love to ask the group next time? Write it here so you don't forget....

Copy down one or two scriptures from the text from the lesson: You may copy the scripture from any of your favorite versions of the Bible.

Lesson Four: Miracles, Signs and Wonders

Miracles, signs and wonders were validation for the early church.

Focus Thought

Jesus fulfilled the promise to grant signs following believers, and He validated the ministry of the early church.

Focus Verse

John 14:12, New King James Version

"Most assuredly, I say to you, he who believes in Me, the works that I do he will do also; and greater works than these he will do, because I go to My Father.

Background Notes for the Group Facilitator

Make sure to have stories of recent miracles, signs, and wonders to share with the group, especially if no one has witnessed any of the above.

Check out Barbara Westberg's recent book, *Stories of the Supernatural: 70 Present-Day Miracles*, available through Amazon.

NOTE: This book would also be a wonderful read-aloud for Sunday school classes and for families at bedtime.

Suggested Meeting Schedule

Open with Prayer

Icebreaker (5 minutes)

Optional Worship Session (5-10 minutes)

Lesson (5-10 minutes)

Discussion (20-30 minutes)

Wrap-up and Reflection (10 minutes)

Share Prayer Needs for the Week

Close with Prayer

Icebreaker (5 minutes)

Tell the group the most amazing supernatural event that you have witnessed: a miracle, a sign or a wonder. The purpose of this is to build the group's faith in the supernatural.

Lesson (5-10 minutes)

Many describe everyday happenings and events as "miracles." Most people who are marketing and label these happenings and events do not even believe in the miraculous power of Jesus Christ. The word "miracle", according to the *Encarta Dictionary*, means an event that appears to be contrary to the laws of nature and is regarded as an act of God or an event or action that is totally amazing, extraordinary, or unexpected.

Some point to the passage in I Corinthians 13:8-11 and say that miracles are not for the church today. If that is the case, then knowledge has vanished as well. Scripture helps us to know that God has all the authority and the power. God is the same yesterday, today, and forever. (See Hebrews 13:8.) His power is the same as it was the day the sun stood still for the children of Israel. (See Joshua 10:13.) God is still God and is still in the business of performing miracles.

There is only one Potentate and only one Almighty. (See I Timothy 6:15 and Revelation 1:8; 4:8.) Jesus Christ is the Savior. (See Luke 2:11 and Isaiah 43:11.) God showed Himself strong throughout the Old and New Testaments with numerous miracles, signs, and wonders. The Bible is our official guide to heaven and is the only official document that we have for understanding God's authority.

God allowed His power to be distributed through the early church. (See Mark 16:17-18.) Believers cast out demons in His name, spoke with new tongues, and laid hands on the sick while they witnessed His miraculous power and glory.

Read the following passages in Acts in reference to the miracle-working power of God: Acts 2:43; 5:12; 6:8; 8:6, 13; 14:3; 15:12; 19:11.

Miracles are divine intervention, not man's invention. Miracles do not have to be analyzed and dissected; believers and unbelievers alike must simply believe. We must believe God for miracles in our midst, more workings of the supernatural power of the Almighty.

Mark 16:17-20, New King James Version

17 And these signs will follow those who believe: In My name they will cast out demons; they will speak with new tongues;

18 they will take up serpents; and if they drink anything deadly, it will by no means hurt them; they will lay hands on the sick, and they will recover."

19 So then, after the Lord had spoken to them, He was received up into heaven, and sat down at the right hand of God.

20 And they went out and preached everywhere, the Lord working with them and confirming the word through the accompanying signs. Amen.

John 14:11-13, NJKV

11 Believe Me that I am in the Father and the Father in Me, or else believe Me for the sake of the works themselves.

12 "Most assuredly, I say to you, he who believes in Me, the works that I do he will do also; and greater works than these he will do, because I go to My Father.

13 And whatever you ask in My name, that I will do, that the Father may be glorified in the Son.

Acts 3:6-8, NKJV

6 Then Peter said, "Silver and gold I do not have, but what I do have I give you: In the name of Jesus Christ of Nazareth, rise up and walk."

7 And he took him by the right hand and lifted him up, and immediately his feet and ankle bones received strength.

8 So he, leaping up, stood and walked and entered the temple with them—walking, leaping, and praising God.

Acts 28:3, 5, NKJV

3 But when Paul had gathered a bundle of sticks and laid them on the fire, a viper came out because of the heat, and fastened on his hand.

5 But he shook off the creature into the fire and suffered no harm.

Discussion (20-30 minutes)

1. Read Mark 16:17-20 and John 14:11-13. Discuss the passage and the words and works listed.
2. Read Acts 3:6-8 and Acts 28:3, 5. Read and discuss the miracles recorded in the passages.
3. Miracles were present in the early New Testament church. Discuss I Corinthians 13:8-11 and what it means by miracles in the New Testament church and the present church.
4. Discuss this quote: "The more we believe in their availability [miracles], the more we will enjoy their possibility."

5. How does the concept of humanism interfere with the validity of the supernatural? Define humanism. (Humanism is defined according to the *Encarta Dictionary*: a system of thought that is based on the values, characteristics, and behavior that are believed to be best in human beings, rather than on any supernatural authority.)

6. Although some would say that God is no longer in the miracle business, the church knows otherwise. Discuss the following reasons why God is still the miracle-working almighty Potentate: People's needs are the same today as they were when He was performing miracles in the early church. God has not changed. (See Malachi 3:6.) Faith in God brings miraculous results.

7. Re-read the passages from Acts at the conclusion of today's lesson. Make a list of all the types of miracles, signs, and wonders. Keep the list for those days when your faith is low and remember that God is the same now as then.

8. Miracles reveal divine intervention. Discuss how more of the supernatural in our lives leads to more faith and more miracles.

9. Discuss with the group any signs of the supernatural that you have witnessed.

Reflection and Wrap-Up

God is the same today as He was in Joshua's day.

Are you expecting God to work in your life? Your local church? Your place of employment?

We are all guilty of expecting the sensational without the faith to believe in the supernatural. What have you been looking for? Miracles, signs, wonders? God works through people.

Are you willing to be a vessel in which God may bring the supernatural to pass?

Do you have the faith to believe God for what you cannot see? Are you willing to believe God for a divine demonstration in your local church services this weekend?

Expect the supernatural in your life and also in your church today.

Take five minutes of this quiet, reflective time to examine your heart while the music plays softly.

Take five minutes for prayer needs.

Close with prayer. Encourage each participant to work through the reflection that follows this page.

Optional: Time of fellowship with light snacks.

Reflection for this week

Write your thoughts about this week's lesson:

Explain your thoughts about any specific points from the discussion:

Perhaps you have thought of another question you'd love to ask the group next time? Write it here so you don't forget....

Copy down one or two scriptures from the text of the lesson: You may copy the scripture from any of your favorite versions of the Bible.

Lesson Five: Supreme over Human Resistance

The followers of Jesus received power

Focus Thought

Jesus fulfilled His promise that His followers would receive power.

Focus Verse

Acts 4:33, New King James Version

And with great power the apostles gave witness to the resurrection of the Lord Jesus. And great grace was upon them all.

Background Notes for the Group Facilitator

Perform some research on the subject of World War II and Adolph Hitler.

Be prepared for the icebreaker which discusses the power of evil over good and the ill-intended intentions of world-wide Supremacy.

Autocracy might be too volatile of a subject for this lesson but fits....

Suggested Meeting Schedule

Open with Prayer

Icebreaker (5 minutes)

Optional Worship Session (5-10 minutes)

Lesson (5-10 minutes)

Discussion (20-30 minutes)

Wrap-up and Reflection (10 minutes)

Share Prayer Needs for the Week

Close with Prayer

Icebreaker (5 minutes)

Discuss how the Allies overcame evil in World War II. Discuss Hitler and how he intended to overtake the world with the ideology of Supremacy.

Lesson (5-10 minutes)

I Corinthians 2:4 states, "And my speech and my preaching were not with persuasive words of human wisdom, but in demonstration of the Spirit and of power,"

All throughout the final days that Jesus was with the disciples, His focus was on the power that was coming in the days ahead. Jesus continued to tell the disciples that when the Holy Ghost came that they would have Holy Ghost power to be witnesses. The disciples were people just like you and me and yet the Holy Ghost moved through them and they accomplished mighty feats in the power of the Spirit.

Although mighty persecution threatened to stop the evangelism efforts of the disciples, the Spirit promised authority over the power of the enemy. (See Luke 10:19.) The disciples and other believers were able to withstand the fiery trials and fierce opposition to the message they were carrying all across the known world.

The disciples worked the field and God gave the increase. The followers of Jesus' message preached, baptized and taught in His name. The Lord had promised signs and wonders to His followers. God did not let the disciples down. They were first-hand witnesses to the power and mighty acts of God in action.

Many came against the church and its evangelistic efforts. King Herod was one who opposed the early church and its message of salvation. Acts 12:1 says that Herod stretched out his hands to harass the church members. Since there is no power on earth greater than God, deliverance was certain and the believers prevailed. (See I John 4:4.)

Some of the disciples found themselves in prisons, stocks and chains. Some were persecuted and even martyred for the gospel. The church responded with fervent prayer for freedom from the opposition.

The church moved forward because of the fervent prayer and evangelistic efforts. Today's church can learn many lessons and find numerous parallels from the early church. Believers will triumph because God is greater than any evil opposition!

Acts 1:8, New King James Version

8 But you shall receive power when the Holy Spirit has come upon you; and you shall be witnesses to Me in Jerusalem, and in all Judea and Samaria, and to the end of the earth."

Luke 24:49, NKJV

49 Behold, I send the Promise of My Father upon you; but tarry in the city of Jerusalem until you are endued with power from on high."

Acts 3:1-9, 12, NKJV

1 Now Peter and John went up together to the temple at the hour of prayer, the ninth hour.

2 And a certain man lame from his mother's womb was carried, whom they laid daily at the gate of the temple which is called Beautiful, to ask alms from those who entered the temple;

3 who, seeing Peter and John about to go into the temple, asked for alms.

4 And fixing his eyes on him, with John, Peter said, "Look at us."

5 So he gave them his attention, expecting to receive something from them.

6 Then Peter said, "Silver and gold I do not have, but what I do have I give you: In the name of Jesus Christ of Nazareth, rise up and walk."

7 And he took him by the right hand and lifted him up, and immediately his feet and ankle bones received strength.

8 So he, leaping up, stood and walked and entered the temple with them—walking, leaping, and praising God.

9 And all the people saw him walking and praising God.

12 So when Peter saw it, he responded to the people: "Men of Israel, why do you marvel at this? Or why look so intently at us, as though by our own power or godliness we had made this man walk?

Discussion (20-30 minutes)

1. Read Acts 3:1-9, 12. Discuss the lame man at the gate called Beautiful, and Peter and John's response.
2. Considering the miracle in Acts 3:1-9, how does a believer explain such a miracle to an unbeliever?
3. Why do miracles exist? Does God have a purpose for miracles?
4. The disciples prayed even more fervently when opposition and persecution arose against them. How could we learn from this example in today's church?
5. Discuss the resistance of King Herod and how that didn't stop Jesus Christ from being born and protected.
6. Discuss the basic foundational principles that kept the early church rock-solid in its beliefs and doctrine.
7. Read Acts 17:31, Psalm 127:1, and Philippians 3:10. Compare the verses and discuss how these were foundational truths to the

disciples' ministry.

8. Consider the transforming power of the Holy Ghost that changed the disciples, both men and women. How can we allow that same Spirit to transform our hearts and lives today?

9. Are there factors in the local church that inhibit the power of the Spirit and the supernatural power moving freely? Discuss.

10. How can we as believers live a more transformed life through the power of the Holy Ghost? What would make our world see the difference?

Reflection and Wrap-Up

Are you living up to the Lord's expectation for your life? Are you Spirit-led in all of your actions, words, and deeds?

Do your coworkers realize that you have a life-transforming power residing within your heart? Are you living beneath your potential in God's kingdom?

What can you do to endure hardship and persecution like the early believers? Are you praying enough?

Are you giving in to the pressure of the Herod's in your life? What does God want to accomplish through your life? Pray and ask God to show you His plan for added power in your life.

Take five minutes of this quiet, reflective time to examine your heart while the music plays softly.

Take five minutes for prayer needs.

Close with prayer. Encourage each participant to work through the reflection that follows this page.

Optional: Time of fellowship with light snacks.

Reflection for this week

Write your thoughts about this week's lesson:

Explain your thoughts about any specific points from the discussion:

Perhaps you have thought of another question you'd love to ask the group next time? Write it here so you don't forget....

Copy down one or two scriptures from the text from the lesson: You may copy the scripture from any of your favorite versions of the Bible.

Lesson Six: Supreme over Mysticism

Power encounters with mysticism demonstrate God's Superiority

Focus Thought

The four power encounters with mysticism recorded in the Book of Acts demonstrate the superiority of God, His Spirit, and His Church.

Focus Verse

I John 4:4, New King James Version

You are of God, little children, and have overcome them, because He who is in you is greater than he who is in the world.

Background Notes for the Group Facilitator

Collect some examples of daily horoscopes and advertisements for places that proclaim palm reading and tarot card reading. You might also want to get some paranormal books from your local library. Some new believers might not yet realize that some of these practices invite spiritual darkness into their lives.

Build a solid support of prayer for your session this week. Be mindful of the spiritual forces at work against this lesson. Light always conquers the darkness!

Suggested Meeting Schedule

Open with Prayer

Icebreaker (5 minutes)

Optional Worship Session (5-10 minutes)

Lesson (5-10 minutes)

Discussion (20-30 minutes)

Wrap-up and Reflection (10 minutes)

Share Prayer Needs for the Week

Close with Prayer

Icebreaker (5 minutes)

What are your thoughts about the craze over the Harry Potter books? Do you think they really are an invitation into the "dark world"?

Have you read the books yourself, or are you just reacting to the anti-Christian hype from Christian groups? Should the books be banned from school libraries? Why or why not?

Lesson (5-10 minutes)

In the Midwest region of the United States, weather confrontations of cold air together with warm air produce thunderstorms and, at times, tornadoes. Once started, these storms cannot be stopped.

In the New Testament, there were several confrontations in the spirit world as well. Simon the sorcerer, Elymas, the servant girl with the spirit of divination, and the seven sons of Sceva are the accounts in the New Testament where the Spirit overcame the evil spirits. (See Acts 8; Acts 13; Acts 16:16-26; Acts 19:13-16.)

Light always prevails over darkness. (See John 1:5.) These confrontations can also be referred to as a spiritual battle. Any battle requires training and procurement of the essential equipment. (Ephesians 6:13-18.) The utmost authority resides in the One, True Spirit and Word of God.

Any time believers attain higher heights in God, they should expect spiritual opposition. Spiritual conflict can signal to believers and today's church that they are on track and a challenge to Satan's kingdom. (See Luke 4:28-29; John 16:33.)

Any individual who thinks any spiritual battle can be fought and won with one's own strength is a fool. That is ludicrous. Believers must fully rely on the Word and the Spirit to engage in any battle.

Just as Midwesterners cannot stop a tornado with their own hands, believers cannot combat the darkness of this world with their own strength.

Acts 8:9-11, 18-19, New King James Version

9 But there was a certain man called Simon, who previously practiced sorcery in the city and astonished the people of Samaria, claiming that he was someone great, 10 to whom they all gave heed, from the least to the greatest, saying, "This man is the great power of God." 11 And they heeded him because he had astonished them with his sorceries for a long time.

18 And when Simon saw that through the laying on of the apostles' hands the Holy Spirit was given, he offered them money, 19 saying, "Give me this power also, that anyone on whom I lay hands may receive the Holy Spirit."

Acts 13:6-12, NKJV

6 Now when they had gone through the island to Paphos, they found a certain sorcerer, a false prophet, a Jew whose name was Bar-Jesus,

7 who was with the proconsul, Sergius Paulus, an intelligent man. This man called for Barnabas and Saul and sought to hear the word of God.

8 But Elymas the sorcerer (for so his name is translated) withstood them, seeking to turn the proconsul away from the faith.

9 Then Saul, who also is called Paul, filled with the Holy Spirit, looked intently at him

10 and said, "O full of all deceit and all fraud, you son of the devil, you

enemy of all righteousness, will you not cease perverting the straight ways of the Lord?

11 And now, indeed, the hand of the Lord is upon you, and you shall be blind, not seeing the sun for a time." And immediately a dark mist fell on him, and he went around seeking someone to lead him by the hand.

12 Then the proconsul believed, when he saw what had been done, being astonished at the teaching of the Lord.

Discussion (20-30 minutes)

Read Acts 8:9-11, 18-19. Discuss Simon's attempt to sway the apostles with money. Was Simon a new believer who was just misguided or someone with ill intentions?

Read Acts 13:6-12. Discuss Elymas, the sorcerer. How was he guilty at standing in the way of a sinner? (See Psalm 1:1.)

1. How did the miracle of Elymas' blindness make the proconsul believe in God even more?
2. In the scripture text, Simon considered the Spirit of God to be a thing, or an object to be owned, controlled, or used. Can you think of other examples of this terrible pattern?
3. Discuss how the Holy Ghost is more powerful than astrology, spiritualism, and Mysticism.
4. Explain how tarot cards, daily horoscopes, and palm reading are of a dark spiritual origin. Why should Christians avoid these practices?
5. How are these modern practices likened to the Old Testament's

high places of the groves, incense, and other pagan practices?

6. The icebreaker mentioned Harry Potter books. How are the events in the New Testament concerning mysticism different than or the same as current awareness about the Harry Potter books? How has mysticism always seemed to be a part of the culture? Are there other popular movies, music, or shows with this same dark message?

7. Consider this statement: For every genuine, there are at least one dozen counterfeits. How does this statement hold with Simon the Sorcerer, the seven sons of Sceva, and the girl with the spirit of divination?

8. What does the church need to be aware of with so many counterfeits? Why is this important?

Reflection and Wrap-Up

How much authority does your spirit have? Will you be the one to cast out the demons, or will you be the one that the demons say, "Who are you?"

There is only one True Spirit. Believers must never fear the darkness because light always triumphs over darkness. A true relationship with Jesus is vital to understanding spiritual authority. Some have not given the Spirit the place it deserves. (See Acts 5:1-10; Leviticus 10:1-2; Leviticus 16:6.)

Believers must possess complete confidence in the workings of the Spirit. The Spirit has all authority over spiritual wickedness and ungodliness. If believers seek God's face in a right relationship, then believers can count on God's Spirit to cover and protect them at all times. (See I John 4:4.)

Take five minutes of this quiet, reflective time to examine your heart while the music plays softly.

Take five minutes for prayer needs.

Close with prayer.

Optional: Time of fellowship with light snacks.

Reflection for this week

Write your thoughts about this week's lesson:

Explain your thoughts about any specific points from the discussion:

Perhaps you have thought of another question you'd love to ask the group next time? Write it here so you don't forget....

Copy down one or two scriptures from the text of the lesson: You may copy the scripture from any of your favorite versions of the Bible.

Lesson Seven: Early Church Became Witnesses of Jesus

The Holy Spirit empowered the believers to become witnesses of Jesus

Focus Thought

The Holy Spirit empowered the believers to become witnesses of Jesus.

Focus Verse

Acts 1:8, New King James Version

But you shall receive power when the Holy Spirit has come upon you; and you shall be witnesses to Me in Jerusalem, and in all Judea and Samaria, and to the end of the earth."

Background Notes for the Group Facilitator

Be prepared with an outline of an evangelistic plan for your group to discuss at the conclusion of this lesson. Any time evangelism is taught, believers should act upon what they have heard. What better way to cement the concept of being a witness than to go out to the streets and put "witness" into practice. Collaborate with your pastor or evangelism leader to apply what has been taught from the previous lessons.

Suggested Meeting Schedule

Open with Prayer

Icebreaker (5 minutes)

Optional Worship Session (5-10 minutes)

Lesson (5-10 minutes)

Discussion (20-30 minutes)

Wrap-up and Reflection (10 minutes)

Share Prayer Needs for the Week

Close with Prayer

Icebreaker (5 minutes)

Have you ever bought a used car? Did you like the salesperson? Why did you buy? How did the salesperson make you feel? Does anyone know the names of the sales techniques?

Lesson (5-10 minutes)

Angels do many things for believers, but they have never presented the gospel to a street person or preached a sermon to a jam-packed church. Just prior to Jesus ascending into heaven, He instructed His followers to be witnesses.

Jesus spent the better part of three years on earth teaching His disciples to be witnesses. Although the disciples had to wait for the Holy Ghost in order to have the resurrecting power in their lives, they understood that they were to be witnesses on that historic day of Jesus' ascension. Witnesses are people whom God calls into His service. The message that the disciples proclaimed was the death, burial, and resurrection of Jesus, and that Jesus was more than just a mere man; He was Emmanuel—God with us. (See Matthew 1:23.)

Jesus instructed His believers to be witnesses in their local city, Jerusalem, Judea, and Samaria, and to all parts of the earth. (See Acts 1:8.) While the disciples were firsthand witnesses to the miracle-working power of God, believers today must possess the same excitement for the miracle-working power of Jesus Christ.

Believers must experience firsthand the supernatural power of God to tell others about the power of God. Believers must fervently pray in order to be filled with the power of God so that unbelievers will say, "What should we do to be saved?" just as the people did in Acts 2. (See Acts 2:37.) Fulfilling the job of being a witness for Jesus should keep the believer praying and full of Holy Ghost power!

The same Spirit that empowered the disciples in the first century still empowers believers today. The same Spirit that propelled followers in the book of Acts propels believers today. Believers are still expected to be witnesses of God's power and glory in today's world.

Acts 1:22, New King James Version

22 beginning from the baptism of John to that day when He was taken up from us, one of these must become a witness with us of His resurrection."

Acts 2:32, NKJV

32 This Jesus God has raised up, of which we are all witnesses.

Acts 3:15, NKJV

15 and killed the Prince of life, whom God raised from the dead, of which we are witnesses.

Acts 4:33, NKJV

33 And with great power the apostles gave witness to the resurrection of the Lord Jesus. And great grace was upon them all.

Acts 5:32, NKJV

32 And we are His witnesses to these things, and so also is the Holy Spirit whom God has given to those who obey Him."

Acts 10:39, NKJV

39 And we are witnesses of all things which He did both in the land of the

Jews and in Jerusalem, whom they killed by hanging on a tree.

Acts 13:31, NKJV

31 He was seen for many days by those who came up with Him from Galilee to Jerusalem, who are His witnesses to the people.

Acts 22:15, NKJV

15 For you will be His witness to all men of what you have seen and heard.

Acts 23:11, NKJV

11 But the following night the Lord stood by him and said, "Be of good cheer, Paul; for as you have testified for Me in Jerusalem, so you must also bear witness at Rome."

Acts 26:16, 22, NKJV

16 But rise and stand on your feet; for I have appeared to you for this purpose, to make you a minister and a witness both of the things which you have seen and of the things which I will yet reveal to you.

22 Therefore, having obtained help from God, to this day I stand, witnessing both to small and great, saying no other things than those which the prophets and Moses said would come—

Discussion (20-30 minutes)

1. Read the scripture passages from the above list. What one word is common to each verse?

2. The disciples evangelized their local area first, then branched out to out-of-town areas. What areas should believers begin with if they follow the disciples' pattern of evangelizing?

3. What does it mean to be a witness?

4. Compare the power of a personal testimony compared to retelling an account of someone else's experience.

5. Why is a written personal testimony so vital to being a witness? What makes a witness believable?

6. Compare Peter hiding in shame and embarrassment following Jesus' death and then boldly proclaiming the truth of the Holy Ghost in Acts 2. What made the difference in Peter?

7. How can the Holy Ghost transform regular people into fiery witnesses for Jesus?

8. True witnesses bring conviction through the moving of the Holy Ghost. Sin brings condemnation. Describe the difference between the two and the importance of not getting the two confused.

9. Salesmen have tactics that persuade unsuspecting consumers into purchasing their products. How should witnesses for the Lord be different? Should witnesses "strong-arm" people into making a step for the Lord? Why or why not?

Reflection and Wrap-Up

Are you being a witness to the power and resurrecting power of Jesus? Why or why not? What is stopping you from proclaiming the power of Jesus?

Have you written down your personal testimony to share with others? If not, why not today? Find some paper and get started! Countless people are praying for a real experience with God. Will you be the one to take salvation to your workplace? School? Neighborhood? Local restaurant? City streets? Street kids? Social media?

Pray and ask Jesus to place a burden to witness deep within your heart and soul. Remember that who God calls, He equips. When God calls you to be a witness, He will give you the tools that you need to be a success!

Take five minutes of this quiet, reflective time to examine your heart while the music plays softly.

Take five minutes for prayer needs.

Close with prayer.

Optional: Time of fellowship with light snacks.

Note: The Appendix gives instructions for writing your testimony.

Reflection for this week

Write your thoughts about this week's lesson:

Explain your thoughts about any specific points from the discussion:

Perhaps you have thought of another question you'd love to ask the group next time? Write it here so you don't forget....

Copy down one or two scriptures from the text from the lesson: You may copy the scripture from any of your favorite versions of the Bible.

Lesson Eight: Witnesses of Jesus Affirm that Jesus is the Messiah & Lord

The early church celebrated the theme "Jesus as Lord and Christ"

Focus Thought

The early church celebrated and rallied about the theme "Jesus as Lord and Christ."

Focus Verse

Acts 2:36, New King James Version

"Therefore let all the house of Israel know assuredly that God has made this Jesus, whom you crucified, both Lord and Christ."

Background Notes for the Group Facilitator

Invite your pastor to come to the group to share his ordination experience and any photos he might have from the milestone.

Suggested Meeting Schedule

Open with Prayer

Icebreaker (5 minutes)

Optional Worship Session (5-10 minutes)

Edification (5-10 minutes)

Discussion (20-30 minutes)

Wrap-up and Reflection (10 minutes)

Share Prayer Needs for the Week

Close with Prayer

Icebreaker (5 minutes)

Describe any ordination service you have attended. This might be an ordination into the ministry or of some other type.

Lesson (5-10 minutes)

Anointing is a concept that had its beginnings in the Old Testament. Both objects and people were anointed with oil to signify the beginning of a special purpose or a special ministry. God's Spirit always accompanied the anointed one as he served. Kings were especially anointed. (See Leviticus 4:3, 5, 16; 6:22; I Samuel 24:6, 10; II Samuel 19:21; 23:1; Isaiah 45:1.)

The word "Messiah" comes from the same root word as our word "anoint". The Messiah was a specially chosen ruler who would bring an end to the suffering of Israel. His main role would be one of Deliverer. John 1:41 states that the Messiah is Jesus Christ or Jehovah-Savior, the Anointed One.

Abraham was in covenant with God, as was David in covenant with God. The covenant that came through David was the promise that a king would come from the line of David. All throughout the Old Testament, the hope of a Messiah was felt. (See Psalm 110; Isaiah 42:1-7; 43:8-10; 50:4-9.) Even when Israel fell to foreign powers, the people never lost hope that their Deliverer would come to save them from destruction.

When the fullness of time came, God sent His Son. (Galatians 4:4.) The apostles taught and preached that Jesus was the long-promised Messiah from the Old Testament. When Peter preached on the Day of Pentecost, part of his message declared, "Jesus was both Lord and Christ [Messiah]" (Acts 2:36). Paul also preached that Jesus was both Lord and Christ, the Messiah. (See Acts 17:3.)

Even Apollos preached that "Jesus is the Christ" in Acts 18:28. The Messiah ruled as King in the hearts of believers. Many people were surprised at the lack of physical or material kingdom. (See Luke 17:21.) Believers understood that the purpose of the kingdom was to restore a lost man to a Savior, i.e., reconciliation. (See I Corinthians 15:20-28; Colossians 1:13;

Romans 14:17.) John 3:3-5 states that the only way to enter the kingdom of God is by the new birth.

Today, believers can seek the kingdom (Matthew 6:33), inherit the kingdom (Matthew 25:34), and enter into it (Luke 16:16). The Messiah has come that believers might live forever with Him in Heaven. Entrance into the kingdom includes repenting of our sins, being baptized in the name of Jesus for the remission of sins, and receiving the gift of the Holy Ghost, evidenced by speaking in other tongues as the Spirit gives the utterance. (See Acts 2:38.) Our King is not willing for anyone to be lost, but for all to come to a knowledge of Him. (See II Peter 3:9.)

Acts 2:25-28, New King James Version

25 For David says concerning Him: 'I foresaw the Lord always before my face, For He is at my right hand, that I may not be shaken. 26 Therefore, my heart rejoiced, and my tongue was glad; Moreover my flesh also will rest in hope. 27 For You will not leave my soul in Hades, Nor will You allow Your Holy One to see corruption.

28 You have made known to me the ways of life; You will make me full of joy in Your presence.'

Acts 2:34-35, NKJV

34 For David did not ascend into the heavens, but he says himself: 'The Lord said to my Lord, "Sit at My right hand, 35 Till I make Your enemies Your footstool." '

Acts 9:3-5, NKJV

3 As he journeyed, he came near Damascus, and suddenly a light shone

around him from heaven. 4 Then he fell to the ground, and heard a voice saying to him, "Saul, Saul, why are you persecuting Me?" 5 And he said, "Who are You, Lord?" Then the Lord said, "I am Jesus, whom you are persecuting. It is hard for you to kick against the goads."

Discussion (20-30 minutes)

1. Read Acts 2:25-28. Discuss how our flesh can rest in hope and how we can be full of joy in the Lord's presence.

2. Read Acts 9:3-5. Saul was witness to a great light. Discuss the powerful manner in which the Lord revealed Himself to Saul. Why did Saul need such a powerful revelation of truth? Do you know anyone like Saul who received a similar revelation?

3. The Jews had to have a revelation that Jesus Christ was the Messiah in the early church. The Gentiles, however, did not know the coming Messiah. Discuss how the apostles had to be wise in presenting the gospel message to both parties.

4. Why do you suppose the Jewish people rejected Jesus as their Messiah?

5. Consider how the disciples referred to Jesus as Jesus Christ after the ascension. Jesus was a common Jewish name in the first century, equivalent to Joshua. Only one Jesus Christ, or Jesus the Messiah, existed then and now! (See John 1:41; 4:25.)

6. Discuss the Old Testament prophecies concerning the coming of the Messiah. Read Isaiah 9:7 and Daniel 2:44; 7:14 as a reference.

7. In our world today, there are many events that point to the return of the Messiah. Discuss these current events across the world.

Reflection and Wrap-Up

Are you awaiting a returning Messiah? Is your heart ready to receive the returning King of Kings? Will you be like the thousands in the early church and scoff and laugh at Christ's return, or will you get your house in order?

Jesus the Christ, the Messiah, will return some glorious (day?) for His church, and believers must not be caught unawares! How many will you be taking to Heaven with you? Have you won anyone to Jesus with this gospel?

Are your children ready to meet their Savior? What steps should you take today if the Lord returned tomorrow?

Take five minutes of this quiet, reflective time to examine your heart while the music plays softly.

Take five minutes for prayer needs.

Close with prayer.

Optional: Time of fellowship with light snacks.

Reflection for this week

Write your thoughts about this week's lesson:

Explain your thoughts about any specific points from the discussion:

Perhaps you have thought of another question you'd love to ask the group next time? Write it here so you don't forget....

Copy down one or two scriptures from the text from the lesson: You may copy the scripture from any of your favorite versions of the Bible.

Lesson Nine: Witnesses of Jesus Affirm His Name

The early church embraced the superior name of Jesus

Focus Thought

The early church embraced and employed the superior name of Jesus.

Focus Verse

Acts 4:12, New King James Version

Nor is there salvation in any other, for there is no other name under heaven given among men by which we must be saved."

Background Notes for the Group Facilitator

Early in the week, choose an individual from the group to research and present the story of Benedict Arnold. The purpose of the story is to show how long a bad name can last and why it's so important to have a good name.

Suggested Meeting Schedule

Open with Prayer

Icebreaker (5 minutes)

Optional Worship Session (5-10 minutes)

Lesson (5-10 minutes)

Discussion (20-30 minutes)

Wrap-up and Reflection (10 minutes)

Share Prayer Needs for the Week

Close with Prayer

Icebreaker (5 minutes)

In advance, ask someone to be prepared to tell the story of Benedict Arnold.

Afterward, ask why a name is so important. How long can a bad name last? In comparison, how long can a good name last?

Lesson (5-10 minutes)

The name of Jesus is fundamental to the church and to believers today. In the New Testament church, the name of Jesus was vital to every activity as well. The early church recognized that its ministry must be encompassed by the power and authority of the name of Jesus: prayer, healing, casting out demons, preaching, and teaching.

Through His name, His presence can be felt. Through His name, anything can be asked, and answers received. The early church believed and practiced Colossians 3:17. Believers understand that names are important.

The three Hebrew boys from the Book of Daniel were given names that reminded them of their covenant with the Lord. One of the first things that Nebuchadnezzar did was change their names to get them to forget their sense of who they were.

Jacob, one of the famous twins, was given a name that meant "supplanter." According to Strong's Concordance, the name Jacob literally means "to seize by the heel." Unfortunately, Jacob lived up to his name with his less-than-honorable methods toward his brother Esau, as well as his father, Isaac.

The early church prayed in Jesus' name. (See Acts 1:14; Acts 1:24-25; Acts 2:42; Acts 3:1; Acts 4:30; Acts 12:5.) Many times, when the church prayed in Jesus' name, signs and wonders followed. The disciples and early church leaders preached in Jesus' name. (See Matthew 23:24; Acts 4:13; Acts 5:28; Acts 5:40.)

Baptism was another fundamental doctrine in the New Testament church. Jesus said that baptism was essential. (See John 3:5.) Jesus also strongly stated that when one believes, they will be baptized. (See Mark 16:16.) In Matthew, Jesus told the disciples to baptize "in the name of the

Father, and of the Son, and of the Holy Ghost" (Matthew 28:19).

The name of Jesus is above every name. It is through His name that we attain healing, deliverance, salvation, and miracles. We know that it is by His name that we are saved. We are baptized in His name, and we should bear witness to His name. We have been called to be witnesses of His name.

Acts 2:21, 38, New King James Version

21 And it shall come to pass That whoever calls on the name of the Lord Shall be saved.'

38 Then Peter said to them, "Repent, and let every one of you be baptized in the name of Jesus Christ for the remission of sins; and you shall receive the gift of the Holy Spirit.

Acts 3:6, 16, NJKV

6 Then Peter said, "Silver and gold I do not have, but what I do have I give you: In the name of Jesus Christ of Nazareth, rise up and walk."

16 And His name, through faith in His name, has made this man strong, whom you see and know. Yes, the faith which comes through Him has given him this perfect soundness in the presence of you all.

Acts 4:7, 10, NKJV

7 And when they had set them in the midst, they asked, "By what power or by what name have you done this?"

10 let it be known to you all, and to all the people of Israel, that by the name of Jesus Christ of Nazareth, whom you crucified, whom God raised

from the dead, by Him this man stands here before you whole.

Acts 5:28, 40-41, NKJV

28 saying, “Did we not strictly command you not to teach in this name? And look, you have filled Jerusalem with your doctrine, and intend to bring this Man’s blood on us!”

40 And they agreed with him, and when they had called for the apostles and beaten them, they commanded that they should not speak in the name of Jesus, and let them go. 41 So they departed from the presence of the council, rejoicing that they were counted worthy to suffer shame for His name.

Discussion (20-30 minutes)

1. Read the scripture passages in Acts 2 and Acts 3. Discuss the instances where the name of Jesus was evoked.

2. Read the scripture passages in Acts 4 and Acts 5. Discuss how the disciples were called before the authorities for using the name of Jesus.

3. Would believers today be strong enough to be called in before the authorities and beaten for the name of Jesus?

4. Why is a name so important?

5. Sometimes, children are given less-than-favorable nicknames. These nicknames sometimes follow them throughout a lifetime. Is this a good practice? Does it begin with good intentions?

6. What are some ways that a person's name influences their behavior and character?

7. Why is it important that believers do all in the name of Jesus?

8. Salvation is wrapped up in Jesus' name. Discuss this fundamental truth.

Reflection and Wrap-Up

Are you bearing witness to Jesus' name? Are you willing to be questioned for the name of Jesus? Are you telling everyone you meet about the name of Jesus and how it liberates and saves?

Do you realize that the name of Jesus is all-powerful? Perhaps we should spend some time reflecting upon the name of Jesus and how it saves, heals, delivers, and teaches us.

Take five minutes of this quiet, reflective time to examine your heart while the music plays softly.

Take five minutes for prayer needs.

Close with prayer.

Optional: Time of fellowship with light snacks.

Reflection for this week

Write your thoughts about this week's lesson:

Explain your thoughts about any specific points from the discussion:

Perhaps you have thought of another question you'd love to ask the group next time? Write it here so you don't forget....

Copy down one or two scriptures from the scripture text from the lesson: You may copy the scripture from any of your favorite versions of the Bible.

Lesson Ten: Witnesses of Jesus Affirm His Resurrection

The resurrection message is central to the gospel message

Focus Thought

Consistently and powerfully declared by the early church, the resurrection message stands as central to the gospel message.

Focus Verse

Acts 26:22-23, New King James Version

22 Therefore, having obtained help from God, to this day I stand, witnessing both to small and great, saying no other things than those which the prophets and Moses said would come—

23 that the Christ would suffer, that He would be the first to rise from the dead, and would proclaim light to the Jewish people and to the Gentiles."

Background Notes for the Group Facilitator

The icebreaker is not intended to be sacrilegious. The quote is for people in your group to consider how life would be or would not be if Jesus Christ had never risen from the dead. Encourage your group to seriously consider the question and its eternal implications.

Suggested Meeting Schedule

Open with Prayer

Icebreaker (5 minutes)

Optional Worship Session (5-10 minutes)

Edification (5-10 minutes)

Discussion (20-30 minutes)

Wrap-up and Reflection (10 minutes)

Share Prayer Needs for the Week

Close with Prayer

Icebreaker (5 minutes)

Ask this absurd question to get your group thinking: What if Jesus Christ had never risen from the dead?

Lesson (5-10 minutes)

While we know assuredly that Jesus Christ rose from the dead and lives even today, the Roman government attempted to cover up the facts of Jesus' resurrection. Hush money was even paid to the Roman guards to say that the disciples had stolen the body of Jesus. (See Matthew 28:11-15.) Although this message did not receive a large audience, some believe it today.

C.S. Lewis said, "If the thing happened, it was the central event in the history of the earth." Scripture records that at least 500 people were witnesses to the resurrection of Jesus and that He was indeed alive. Some of the disciples were put to their deaths for believing in Christ. Would they have gone to their deaths if the story had been fabricated?

Everyone who has ever lived has also died or will die eventually. (See Ecclesiastes 9:4-6.) The disciples were witnesses to Jesus' death and were no doubt in much shock as they had seen Jesus Christ Himself raise the dead several times! Little did they know that in three days, they would be witness to Him very much alive in their midst.

Many in Jerusalem witnessed the miracle of Jesus' resurrection. There were eyewitnesses to His empty tomb: Mary Magdalene, Mary the mother of James, Joanna, Salome, and others. (See Matthew 28; Mark 16; Luke 24; John 20.)

There were also witnesses in the city. (See Acts 13:31.) Jesus appeared in the room where the disciples and other followers were gathered. (See John 20:19-20 and Luke 24:39-43.)

There are many scriptures concerning the resurrection of Jesus Christ. Some are listed here for reference: I Timothy 3:16; Luke 24:50-52; Matthew 12:40; Jonah 2:2. Without a doubt, the Lord rose on the third day and lives forevermore.

Acts 26:6-7, 22-29, New King James Version

6 And now I stand and am judged for the hope of the promise made by God to our fathers.

7 To this promise our twelve tribes, earnestly serving God night and day, hope to attain. For this hope's sake, King Agrippa, I am accused by the Jews.

22 Therefore, having obtained help from God, to this day I stand, witnessing both to small and great, saying no other things than those which the prophets and Moses said would come—

23 that the Christ would suffer, that He would be the first to rise from the dead, and would proclaim light to the Jewish people and to the Gentiles."

24 Now as he thus made his defense, Festus said with a loud voice, "Paul, you are beside yourself! Much learning is driving you mad!"

25 But he said, "I am not mad, most noble Festus, but speak the words of truth and reason.

26 For the king, before whom I also speak freely, knows these things; for I am convinced that none of these things escapes his attention, since this thing was not done in a corner.

27 King Agrippa, do you believe the prophets? I know that you do believe."

28 Then Agrippa said to Paul, "You almost persuade me to become a Christian."

29 And Paul said, "I would to God that not only you, but also all who hear me today, might become both almost and altogether such as I am, except for these chains."

Discussion (20-30 minutes)

1. Read the scripture passage Acts 26:6-7, 22-29. Discuss the resurrection of Jesus Christ in light of this passage.
2. Did King Agrippa believe Paul concerning the resurrection? How do you know?
3. Read John 11:25. Compare the resurrections of Lazarus and Jesus Christ. Jesus showed great power when He called Lazarus from the tomb, but showed even greater power when He emerged from His own tomb very much alive. Discuss.
4. Imagine living in the first century and continually persuading neighbors and family members that Jesus was the Christ, the Messiah. Discuss what credibility was added to that argument when Jesus arose from the dead and was seen by eyewitnesses.
5. Canadian scientist, G. B. Hardy, offered the following observation: "There are but two essential requirements: First, has anyone cheated death and proved it? Second: Is it available to me? Here is the complete record. Confucius' tomb—occupied. Buddha's tomb—occupied. Mohamed's tomb—occupied. Jesus' tomb—empty. Argue as you will. There is no point in following a loser." Discuss this powerful quote.

6. Believers have eternal hope through Jesus Christ's resurrection. Read I Corinthians 15:19-23 and Titus 3:7 and discuss the scriptures in light of the hope available to all believers.
7. If one were to read all the eyewitness accounts from the New Testament, which account is the most convincing? Why?
8. Jesus chose Mary Magdalene to be the first eyewitness to the resurrection and the empty tomb. Why do you suppose she was chosen as the first eyewitness?
9. How do you suppose Pilate reacted when he heard the news that Jesus was alive after being dead in the tomb for three days? How did other unbelievers react?
10. How are you living in victory? What effect has the resurrection had on you as a believer?

Reflection and Wrap-Up

Jesus Christ was dead, buried, and rose on the third day. Jesus Christ's resurrecting power is still yet coming back to claim a bride just as He said He would before He ascended into Heaven. (See I Thessalonians 4:16-18; John 14:1-3.)

He is coming for the living and the dead in Christ. What a promise to know that Jesus is coming for His people someday soon!

What are you doing to celebrate the resurrection of Jesus Christ? Do you only think about it on Easter Sunday?

Why would it be important to reflect upon the greatest miracle ever known to man? Why wait for Easter Sunday? Celebrate today that Jesus lives forever!

Take five minutes of this quiet, reflective time to examine your heart while the music plays softly.

Take five minutes for prayer needs.

Close with prayer.

Optional: Time of fellowship with light snacks.

Reflection for this week

Write your thoughts about this week's lesson:

Explain your thoughts about any specific points from the discussion:

Perhaps you have thought of another question you'd love to ask the group next time. Write it here so you don't forget..

Copy down one or two scriptures from the text from the lesson: You may copy the scripture from any of your favorite versions of the Bible.

Lesson Eleven: The Early Church in Growth & Geographic Expansion

The early church exploded in growth that crossed both geographic and cultural barriers

Focus Thought

Ignited with passion and mission, the early church exploded in growth and expansion that crossed both geographic and cultural barriers.

Focus Verse

Acts 19:10, New King James Version

And this continued for two years, so that all who dwelt in Asia heard the word of the Lord Jesus, both Jews and Greeks.

Background Notes for the Group Facilitator

Conduct research on Chief Standing Bear, a Ponca nation chief. He was instrumental in tearing down prejudices among the Ponca Indians and U.S. government in Nebraska, South Dakota, and Oklahoma. You might consider asking someone from the group to perform the research and presentation.

Suggested Meeting Schedule

Open with Prayer Icebreaker (5 minutes)

Optional Worship Session (5-10 minutes)

Lesson (5-10 minutes)

Discussion (20-30 minutes)

Wrap-up and Reflection (10 minutes)

Share Prayer Needs for the Week

Close with Prayer

Icebreaker (5 minutes)

Present a short synopsis on the life and testimony of Chief Standing Bear. When finished, ask these questions:

Did Chief Standing Bear act rashly or violently? Did the court system treat the Chief like a real person? What did Chief Standing Bear tell the courtroom about the color of his blood and his skin, and the color of the judge's skin? What significance does that have in history?

Lesson (5-10 minutes)

Acts 1:8 issued an edict to the disciples. Jesus told them to be witnesses at home and in distant lands. They were also to wait in Jerusalem until they were filled with power from on high. On the Day of Pentecost, they were filled with the promise and the power that Jesus spoke of that momentous day. The believers started in Jerusalem and followed the Holy Ghost from there to the "end of the earth."

Jesus chose Jerusalem to be the birthplace of the church. Psalm 48:2 states that Jerusalem was the "city of the great King." Psalm 22:27-28 mandates that "all the ends of the world shall remember and turn unto the Lord..." All the kingdoms of the earth belong to God and will someday all bow down and worship Him as King. (See Psalm 66:4.)

The New Testament church grew beyond the communities of the Jewish people and beyond the Samaritan communities. The cultural aspects of the church were expanded, as well as the geographical ones. The Jews rejected the Samaritans' rebuilding the Temple, and the Samaritans became a closed community, but the power of the Holy Ghost transcended all cultural barriers. (See John 4:21-24.)

The Gentiles also received the Upper Room experience. Peter traveled to Joppa and visited the home of Simon the tanner. The customs of the day did not look favorably upon the occupation of a tanner. Nevertheless, Peter stayed at Simon's home and brought Jesus Christ to the Gentiles. (See Acts 15:16-17.) The Ethiopian also received the revelation of baptism in the name of Jesus through Philip. (See Acts 8.)

God was sending the Holy Ghost upon all cultures and locations. The Lord even sent Peter a vision three times to convince him to share the gospel with a Gentile. Finally, Peter went to Cornelius and told him about the Holy Ghost. Cornelius and his household were all baptized in the name of Jesus Christ for the remission of their sins and were also filled with the Holy Ghost. (See Acts 10.)

Just as in the early church, there is no room for prejudice in God's kingdom. We have a dictate to take the gospel across the street and around the world, no matter what the cultural barriers or geographical distance.

Acts 1:8, New King James Version

8 But you shall receive power when the Holy Spirit has come upon you; and you shall be witnesses to Me in Jerusalem, and in all Judea and Samaria, and to the end of the earth."

Acts 6:7, NKJV

7 Then the word of God spread, and the number of the disciples multiplied greatly in Jerusalem, and a great many of the priests were obedient to the faith.

Acts 9:31, NKJV

31 Then the churches throughout all Judea, Galilee, and Samaria had peace and were edified. And walking in the fear of the Lord and in the comfort of the Holy Spirit, they were multiplied

Acts 12:24, NKJV

24 But the word of God grew and multiplied.

Acts 19:20, NKJV

20 So the word of the Lord grew mightily and prevailed.

Acts 28:31, NKJV

31 preaching the kingdom of God and teaching the things which concern the Lord Jesus Christ with all confidence, no one forbidding him

Discussion (20-30 minutes)

1. Read the passages above from Acts. Discuss how the gospel was spread geographically and culturally.
2. Jesus Christ wanted there to be no barriers, either geographical or cultural. The church has a mandate to reach all people everywhere with this gospel. Discuss this mandate.
3. The early church had to set aside its prejudices to follow God's leading. Discuss Peter lodging at Simon the tanner's home and Philip ministering to the Ethiopian. Discuss these instances.
4. The church is at times closed-minded to any ethnic groups and cultures that it fears or of which it has limited knowledge. Discuss why this is so.
5. How does the church open its doors and its mind to embrace all cultures and reach them with the gospel?

6. Some say it is human nature to fear the things you know little or nothing about. That fear leads to prejudices, misunderstandings, and hatred.
7. How does that fear and prejudice lead to barriers for the gospel? What can be done to end all fear of other cultures and stop all prejudices?
8. Discuss this quote by Chief Standing Bear: "That hand is not the color of yours, but if I pierce it, I shall feel pain. If you pierce your hand, you also feel pain. The blood that will flow from mine will be the same color as yours. I am a man. The same God made us both."
9. What is the purpose of your local church in these end times?
10. Discuss ways that your local church can embrace all cultures and geographical challenges within your city.

Reflection and Wrap-Up

What fears do you have of other cultures? What deep-seated prejudices do you carry against others? Why? Is that a learned behavior on your part, or were you taught to fear and hate as a child?

How can you reach those cultures that you were taught to despise and disrespect with your words and your actions?

What can you do to make sure your local church does its part to evangelize your lost city, your lost state, your lost world?

Take five minutes of this quiet, reflective time to examine your heart while the music plays softly.

Take five minutes for prayer needs.

Close with prayer.

Optional: Time of fellowship with light snacks.

Reflection for this week

Write your thoughts about this week's lesson:

Explain your thoughts about any specific points from the discussion:

Perhaps you have thought of another question you'd love to ask the group next time. Write it here so you don't forget.

Copy down one or two scriptures from the text of the lesson: You may copy the scripture from any of your favorite versions of the Bible.

Lesson Twelve: The Omniscient God

The early church is a witness to mankind

Focus Thought

The early church stands as a glorious God-given miracle to mankind.

Focus Verse

Acts 2:47, New King James Version

Praising God and having favor with all the people. And the Lord added to the church daily those who were being saved.

Suggested Meeting Schedule

Open with Prayer

Icebreaker (5 minutes)

Optional Worship Session (5-10 minutes)

Lesson (5-10 minutes)

Discussion (20-30 minutes)

Wrap-up and Refection (10 minutes)

Share Prayer Needs for the Week

Close with Prayer

Icebreaker (5 minutes)

What is a secret about you that you do not mind sharing with the group? Maybe you have a secret to success in your devotional time, or maybe you have a recipe secret that you would be willing to share with us? Maybe you have a secret place that you get the best deals and sales but you have not shared that with your brothers and sisters?

Lesson (5-10 minutes)

The early church was wildly successful on their quest to build a church in the name of Jesus Christ. Many have been successful in this life, such as Jonas Salk, inventor of the polio vaccine, Roger Bannister, who broke the four-minute mile record, and Neil Armstrong, who placed the first footprint on the moon's surface. These will leave a legacy that will always shout their achievements.

None can compare to God and His wonderful works! (See Psalm 40:5.) Just imagine for a moment the wonder of a rainbow, the miracle of a newborn baby, or the momentous power of Niagara Falls. Only God can accomplish those breathtaking achievements.

The church is another one of God's creations. He thought out the structure, the building, and the destiny of the church. We can do our best, but it is God alone who builds the church. (See Matthew 16:18; Psalm 127:1.)

The church was bought, or redeemed, by Jesus Christ. (See I Corinthians 6:20.) The early church had several secrets to its success. In just a few short years, the group of believers had turned "...the world upside down..." (Acts 17:6).

These are the five secrets to their success:

- Apostles' Doctrine (Acts 2:42),
- Fellowship-Community (Hebrews 10:25),
- Ministry and service to one another (See Galatians 5:13; See Ephesians 4:32; Romans 15:14; I Thessalonians 4:18; 5:11; Hebrews 3:13; John 15:12.)
- Worship to God (Acts 2:47), and
- Evangelism of the lost (Acts 2:47).

The church consists of individuals who care for each other as well as guide the lost to Jesus Christ through intentional discipleship. Believers must engage in daily lifestyle evangelism and commit to a lifestyle that closely follows the dictates of scripture.

Matthew 16:15-18, New King James Version

15 He said to them, "But who do you say that I am?"

16 Simon Peter answered and said, "You are the Christ, the Son of the living God."

17 Jesus answered and said to him, "Blessed are you, Simon Bar-Jonah, for flesh and blood has not revealed this to you, but My Father who is in heaven.

18 And I also say to you that you are Peter, and on this rock I will build My church, and the gates of Hades shall not prevail against it.

Acts 2:42-47, NKJV

42 And they continued steadfastly in the apostles' doctrine and fellowship, in the breaking of bread, and in prayers.

43 Then fear came upon every soul, and many wonders and signs were done through the apostles.

44 Now all who believed were together, and had all things in common,

45 and sold their possessions and goods, and divided them among all, as anyone had need.

46 So, continuing daily with one accord in the temple, and breaking bread from house to house, they ate their food with gladness and simplicity of heart,

47 praising God and having favor with all the people. And the Lord added to the church daily those who were being saved.

Discussion (20-30 minutes)

1. Read Matthew 16:15-18. Discuss what Peter said to Jesus and Jesus' response. What rock was Jesus Christ referring to in verse 18?
2. Read Acts 2:42-47. The disciples did many notable feats in this passage. Make a mental list and discuss the many things in which the disciples participated.
3. Why is Jesus Christ so passionate about His church? Why should we be so passionate about His church, our church?
4. Consider the five areas that were considered secrets to the early church's success. What areas should we seek to improve, both personally and corporately? All five areas that were mentioned above are important. Discuss what areas need more attention or are perhaps more vital than others.
5. For a church to continue to grow, the members must be committed to lifestyle evangelism. Discuss what lifestyle evangelism means and why it is not the pastor's responsibility to be the only soul winner in the church.
6. In your opinion, are the members of your local church, including you, proficient at explaining the doctrines of the Bible? Why or why not?
7. What is a secret sauce of your local church that you want your community to know about? How do you get the word out?
8. If everyone in your local church were just like you, what kind of church would your church be?

Reflection and Wrap-Up

The last question is a thought-provoking question. We sometimes criticize the church and its members and forget that we are there also. We are collectively the church of Jesus Christ.

What do you individually contribute to your local assembly? Are there ministries the pastor is desperate to begin, but cannot because of a lack of commitment or involvement? What are you doing about that?

As an individual, are you pleasing God with your church attendance and contribution to the church, both financially and with your time? What areas do you need to work on to make yourself better so that, in turn, your local church can be better?

There is a saying that if everyone swept their own sidewalk, the whole world would be clean. That is true in the church body as well. Let us all sweep our hearts and lives so our church becomes better!

Take five minutes of this quiet, reflective time to examine your heart while the music plays softly.

Take five minutes for prayer needs.

Close with prayer.

Optional: Time of fellowship with light snacks.

Reflection for this week

Write your thoughts about this week's lesson:

Explain your thoughts about any specific points from the discussion:

Perhaps you have thought of another question you'd love to ask the group next time? Write it here so you don't forget.

Copy down one or two scriptures from the text from the lesson: You may copy the scripture from any of your favorite versions of the Bible.

Lesson Thirteen: Christianity on Trial

Christianity was not eliminated, but is yet viable even today

Focus Thought

Rather than being eliminated in a culture that resisted new religions, Christianity appears as the viable, surviving outgrowth of the disintegrating Jewish faith.

Focus Verse

Acts 26:31-32, New King James Version

31 and when they had gone aside, they talked among themselves, saying, “This man is doing nothing deserving of death or chains.”

32 Then Agrippa said to Festus, “This man might have been set free if he

had not appealed to Caesar."

Background Notes for the Group Facilitator

In advance, ask your pastor to prepare a list of ministries or areas of evangelism in case your group needs help with these areas.

Perhaps ask your Pastor to come and share his vision with the group concerning evangelism for your area. Support your pastor and his vision. There is only one vision for your city that God is blessing, that of your pastor.

Suggested Meeting Schedule

Open with Prayer

Icebreaker (5 minutes)

Optional Worship Session (5-10 minutes)

Lesson (5-10 minutes)

Discussion (20-30 minutes)

Wrap-up and Reflection (10 minutes)

Share Prayer Needs for the Week

Close with Prayer

Icebreaker (5 minutes)

Tell of your experience in a courtroom. Have you called to be a witness? Have you been called to jury duty? Have you accompanied someone to court as their moral support? Tell about your experiences in a courtroom.

Lesson (5-10 minutes)

The Book of Acts shows a snapshot of life in the New Testament church. The writer, Luke, portrayed the happenings of the church against a backdrop of historical contexts. Readers have an idea of the emperors, officials, governors, and kings from Luke's perspective.

When the church began on the Day of Pentecost, all the believers were Jewish. Not until Cornelius was converted was a Gentile born into the church. Most of the concerns or problems dealt mostly with Jewish customs, traditions, and doctrine. Peter had to become the manager for the church, keeping everyone happy and supporting the Gentiles and the Samaritans as they entered the church. Even after Peter returned from Caesarea and the Roman centurion, the elders of the church questioned Peter when he returned, because of his involvement with a Gentile. (See Acts 11:1-18.)

Some of the Pharisees converted and confessed that Jesus Christ was the Messiah after some convincing testimony from the believers. This group of Jewish scholars even contributed to the development of the church and its doctrines. (See Acts 2:25-36; 3:12-26; 4:8-12; 7:2-53; 26:1-29.)

Written by Luke, the book of Acts focused primarily on the conversion of the Gentiles. While Paul focused on his Jewish heritage, Luke focused more on the evangelism of the Gentiles and building the foundation of the church. Paul preached to Gentiles and seemed to be the ambassador to the Gentile people.

Many people were confused about the new church that was born in the book of Acts. The Romans thought the church was strange because their God was invisible and their worship practices odd.

God had the right people in the right places to accomplish the work that He wanted. God called every tribe and tongue to His church then and is still calling every nationality today. Will believers meet the challenge that was issued in Acts to preach and teach this gospel to every creature?

Acts 26:19-32, New King James Version

19 "Therefore, King Agrippa, I was not disobedient to the heavenly vision,

20 but declared first to those in Damascus and in Jerusalem, and throughout all the region of Judea, and then to the Gentiles, that they should repent, turn to God, and do works befitting repentance.

21 For these reasons, the Jews seized me in the temple and tried to kill me.

22 Therefore, having obtained help from God, to this day I stand, witnessing both to small and great, saying no other things than those which the prophets and Moses said would come—

23 that the Christ would suffer, that He would be the first to rise from the dead, and would proclaim light to the Jewish people and to the Gentiles."

24 Now as he thus made his defense, Festus said with a loud voice, "Paul, you are beside yourself! Much learning is driving you mad!"

25 But he said, "I am not mad, most noble Festus, but speak the words of truth and reason.

26 For the king, before whom I also speak freely, knows these things; for I

am convinced that none of these things escapes his attention, since this thing was not done in a corner.

27 King Agrippa, do you believe the prophets? I know that you do believe."

28 Then Agrippa said to Paul, "You almost persuade me to become a Christian."

29 And Paul said, "I would to God that not only you, but also all who hear me today, might become both almost and altogether such as I am, except for these chains."

30 When he had said these things, the king stood up, as well as the governor and Bernice and those who sat with them;

31 and when they had gone aside, they talked among themselves, saying, "This man is doing nothing deserving of death or chains."

32 Then Agrippa said to Festus, "This man might have been set free if he had not appealed to Caesar."

Discussion (20-30 minutes)

1. Read Acts 26:19-32. Discuss how Paul preached Jesus to Festus and King Agrippa. What was their response? Were they converted?
2. Judaism influenced Christianity. Describe how this transpired.
3. If Christianity were on trial today, do we have enough evidence to convict it as real? Explain and use the scriptures that you have learned through this quarter's study.
4. The book of Acts records two major speeches: Stephen before

he was stoned and Paul before Agrippa. Compare the two and discuss. (See Acts 6-7; Acts 25-26.)

5. Describe why the book of Acts is so important to the church today. Give several compelling reasons.

6. Is the church of today what God desires? Would a court find the church guilty of serving each other and of loving all nations? Why or why not?

7. How are our national and world governments similar to the Roman government of the New Testament church? How are the two different?

8. The entire continent of Asia had heard the gospel within a space of 15 years from the inception of the church. Comparatively, how is the twenty-first-century church doing?

9. How could the church be more effective in spreading the gospel and turning our world upside down?

Reflection and Wrap-Up

What role do you have in personal evangelism? Are you zealous in seeing people converted to Jesus Christ?

Are you complacent about the size of the church today, or do you desire to see the church multiply mightily?

This week, write an individual plan of action to reach the lost in your community, your city, your state, your nation. What are some easy ways you could practice lifestyle evangelism in your daily routine?

Pray that God will anoint and bless your efforts. Pray that you will get involved with what God is already blessing.

Bless your church and your pastor today with faithfulness and loyalty to this great gospel!

Take five minutes of this quiet, reflective time to examine your heart while the music plays softly.

Take five minutes for prayer needs.

Close with prayer.

Optional: Time of fellowship with light snacks.

Reflection for this week:

Write your thoughts about this week's lesson:

Explain your thoughts about any specific points from the discussion:

Perhaps you have thought of another question you'd love to ask the group next time? Write it here so you don't forget.

Copy down one or two scriptures from the scripture from the lesson: You may copy the scripture from any of your favorite versions of the Bible.

Appendix

Additional Materials

The Value of Your Testimony

- It is unique. There are no others just like it! If you don't tell it, no one will know!
- It is personal and easy to understand.
- You are the authority on it. It is impossible to argue with.
- People love to hear personal stories and they remember them.
- People can relate to it. It builds a relational bridge.
- In our postmodern world, it may be your most effective witness.

Four Parts of Your Testimony

1. What my life was like before I received the Holy Ghost (spend least amount of time on this one, maybe 10%).

2. How I realized I needed something (more time on this part, maybe 25%).

3. How I believed and received my new birth experience (even more part on this part, maybe 35%).

4. The difference it has made in my life (spend most of your time on this part, maybe 60%).

Write It Down

Using the questions and percentages above, write your testimony: either on paper or digitally. Spend time in prayer about your testimony. Ask friends and mentors to read it and give constructive feedback.

Next, create an "elevator version" of your testimony. This is the one that could be given in 30-45 seconds. If the person with whom you're sharing your testimony wants to hear more, then you may give your entire story!

Once you have both versions, **elevator and long play**, ask the Lord to give you daily opportunities to share with people who are hungry to hear the gospel.

Perhaps your group could have a testimony celebration night! Everyone could share their testimonies or a few testimonies could be scheduled for each meeting. Friends could be invited to hear the testimonies of the gathered group. Who knows how many hungry souls are just waiting for an opportunity to hear your salvation story?

Other ideas include a YouTube channel for your group testimonies, dedicated social media for the testimonies, or time set aside at your local assembly for the house group testimonies.

What ideas do you have for the distribution of the group's testimonies? Brainstorm your ideas here:

> "We won't really become change agents for Christ just by going to church on Sundays. We will have to make some "**on purpose**" life choices and then change our priorities and our behaviors. Only then can God transform us and use us to change the world. (Rich Stearns, p. 245, The Hole in the Gospel)

Notes

Books referenced in this volume:

Cashin, W. E. (2011). Effective classroom discussions. IDEA Paper number 49

Stearns, Rich. *The Hole in Our Gospel: What Does God Expect of Us? The Answer That Changed My Life and Might Just Change the World.* Thomas Nelson. 2009.

Westberg, Barbara. *Stories of the Supernatural: 70 Present-Day Miracles.* Amazon. 2023.

About the Author

Valeria holds a Bachelor of Science in Elementary Education and brings more than 27 years of experience in public education in the state of Oklahoma. She also earned a Master's of Education with a concentration in Curriculum and Instruction, equipping her with extensive expertise in teaching, leadership development, and educational design. For seven years, she served as an adjunct professor at Northern Oklahoma College, investing in the academic and personal growth of future educators and leaders.

In addition to her educational career, Valeria has dedicated over 35 years to ministry alongside her husband. Throughout those years, she has faithfully served as a pastor's wife, musician, Sunday school teacher, youth teacher, mentor, and leader, impacting multiple generations through discipleship and Christian education.

Valeria is curriculum writer for PPH, PRG, and has also developed curriculum and a textbook for GATS Faculty Development with Global Missions of the United Pentecostal Church International. Her passion for equipping the next generation through leadership development led her to co-initiate the Oklahoma NextGen Leader Program, designed to identify, equip, and empower the next generation of leaders. She continues to mentor individuals in both ministry and education, encouraging others to discover purpose, pursue healing and lead with authenticity.

Valeria and husband Rick, are the co-founders of a 501(c)3 non-profit organization, Kingdom Advance Ministry. This non-profit ministry exists to equip and strengthen leaders and local churches.

They also raise their own funds to travel extensively across the U.S. and internationally to equip ministry, business leaders, and young adults.

Kingdom Advance Ministry may be scheduled for training sessions and equipping of teachers, strengthening local churches, ministry staff, and business leaders around the globe.

Valeria blogs weekly at Kingdom Advance's website, Transformative Teachings
Reach out to Valeria at hughes@kingdomadvanceministry.com.

Feel free to use the code **Thanks40** for 40% discount for resources at the Kingdom Advance website

Kingdom Advance Linktr.ee

Scan to purchase books from Amazon

Audible audio book read and recorded by the author

Scan the QR to participate in an anonymous survey by the author about the debilitating hindrance of shame

Thank you for your purchase! We appreciate your support.

Be watching for the next book in this small group series!

www.ingramcontent.com/pod-product-compliance
Lightning Source LLC
LaVergne TN
LVHW040221110826
845146LV00005B/1363

* 9 7 9 8 9 8 9 2 8 9 8 4 4 *